HOW TO BE HAPPY & FLOURISH IN A

SEASON

—— of ——

CHANGE

30-DAY SURVIVAL GUIDE

HOW TO BE HAPPY & FLOURISH IN A

SEASON

—— of ——

CHANGE

30-DAY SURVIVAL GUIDE

I am the Vine; you are the branches. Whoever lives in Me and I in him bears much (abundant) fruit. However, apart from Me [cut off from vital union with Me] you can do nothing.

JOHN 15:5

"I love this scripture because it reminds me that God doesn't expect me to change on my own. He is the power source and gives us the grace and strength we need to do what's right and make changes in our lives." —Joyce

DEAR FRIEND,

Change is a natural, ongoing part of life. And oftentimes, it isn't easy to go through. Whatever change you face—a new career, a cross-country move, a change in friendships, a relational change, new season of life—it can test your faith and cause you to worry, be anxious, stressed-out or be afraid.

But the truth is, it doesn't have to be this way. You can actually be happy, flourish and thrive in seasons of change. You can find yourself closer to God in these times than you've ever been before!

I know from personal experience that going through seasons of change can be difficult. That's why I've put together this survival guide that will help you do *more* than just survive them. I want to help you learn how you can be happy and thrive in any season!

If you're going through a challenging time of change today—whether it's big or small—I want to encourage you to go through this booklet for the next 30 days. Take a few minutes each day to seek God and trust Him during this time. If you'll do that, I believe you can begin to experience a closer relationship with God and have more peace and joy than ever before.

As you use these daily devotions, you'll discover that God does some of His best work during the difficult times. So take heart. God is with you. He has promised never to leave you. And He has a great plan in store for your life!

DAY 1

GRACE IS GOD'S POWER coming to us freely, enabling us to do with ease what we could never do on our own.

There is nothing more powerful than grace. In fact, everything in the Bible—salvation, renewed strength, personal relationship with God, healing in our souls and bodies, and all of the victory we have in our daily lives—is based upon it.

> *Strengthened by grace,*
> *there is no challenge in your life*
> *too big for you to face!*

If you will allow the grace of God to have full reign in your life, you can find joy in every season of change.

God will give you the strength you need to not just survive, but to flourish and thrive through any circumstance.

SCRIPTURE TO MEDITATE ON TODAY

He said to me, "My grace is sufficient for you, for My strength is made perfect in weakness...."

2 CORINTHIANS 12:9 NKJV

DAY 2

THERE ARE SOME THINGS you *can* control in life—your choice of job, who your friends are, what you do for fun. And there are others you *can't*—what people say and do, that flat tire on the way to work, certain times and seasons of change.

How you react to those things you *can't* control affects your level of happiness and overall quality of life.

> *If you'll learn to shrug off things you can't control, you'll find increased contentment, peace and joy.*

"Shrug therapy" isn't indifference; it simply means you acknowledge there is nothing you can do at that moment to change the situation. Rather than getting upset, cast your care on the Lord (see 1 Peter 5:7) and let Him take control of the things you cannot.

How can you practice "shrug therapy?" What is happening in your life that you need to give completely to God?

Financial - Security!
Learning - wrighting -N-
reading with Halley.
And changes.

DAY 3

FOR SHE KEPT SAYING, *If I only touch His garments, I shall be restored to health* (Mark 5:28).

This woman in Mark chapter 5, who fought her way through the crowd, touched the hem of Jesus' garment and received her healing, did something amazing . . . she "kept saying."

She kept saying to herself, *Jesus can heal me.* She kept saying to herself, *I'm not going to give up.* She kept saying to herself, *Just a little bit farther.*

> *Now let me ask you a question:*
> *What is the thing you keep*
> *saying to yourself?*

In the midst of change, uncertainty or difficulty, don't rehearse the problem; keep saying God's promises until you touch the hem of His garment and see those promises fulfilled.

Take a moment now to look up these scriptures and declare out loud that God is going to see you through the challenge you are facing:

PHILIPPIANS 4:13

PSALM 57:7

MATTHEW 19:26

DAY 4

WHEN YOU TRUST GOD regardless of the circumstances around you, you learn to relax and enjoy life.

You don't have to go through each day worrying and trying to figure out how to solve all your problems. Think about all the things you have worried about in your life . . . and how they worked out. That should help you see that worry is a waste of time and energy.

> *Let me encourage you to stop complicating your life by trying to figure everything out.*

Just admit that you don't have all the answers, but you know the One who does. Psalm 143:8 and

Proverbs 3:5-6 promise that He will show you the way you should go and give you the answers you need. Trust God and experience a new level of joy in your life.

Write your own personal prayer of trust in God for today . . .

That I am doing my best with Haley. And everything will be O.K and work out

DAY 5

IF YOU LOOK BACK over your life, you will see that the deepest personal growth happens during the hardest times. Then later, in the easier times, you enjoy what you have gained.

> ***In other words, you can't have the perks without the works!***

This is a basic principle of life. For example, if you work all week, then you receive your paycheck and enjoy the weekend off. If you exercise, eat right and take care of yourself, then you enjoy a healthy body.

Hebrews 12:11 (NKJV) says: *Now no chastening seems to be joyful for the present, but painful; nevertheless, afterward it yields the peaceable fruit of righteousness to those who have been trained by it.*

To be truly victorious, we must grow to the place where we are not afraid of hard times, because it is during these hard times that we grow the most and become better through them.

QUESTION TO CONSIDER . . .

What is God teaching me through this season of transition and change?

DAY 6

NOT THAT I HAVE now attained [this ideal], or have already been made perfect, but I press on to lay hold of (grasp) and make my own, that for which Christ Jesus (the Messiah) has laid hold of me and made me His own (Philippians 3:12).

In this passage of Scripture, the apostle Paul talks about the importance of perseverance. He is basically saying, *I'm going to keep moving forward . . . no matter what.*

> *I've discovered that often the most spiritual thing you can do is simply refuse to give up.*

You may not have all the answers . . . you may feel tired and confused . . . you may wish the situation was different . . . But if you'll just keep pressing on, God is going to give you the strength you need to make it through.

WISE WORDS

By perseverance the snail reached the ark.

—CHARLES SPURGEON

DAY 7

YOU MAY BE HURTING badly and crying out for help. If that's where you are today, I have good news: God wants to help you! You simply need to be *willing* to receive the help you need from Him.

No matter how much we may want or need help, we can only receive it when we choose to do things God's way.

> *If we will submit to His way, everything will work out.*

Remember, God's way is always best. If He is asking you to forgive that person . . . forgive. If He is guiding you to take a step of faith . . . go for it. If He is speaking to you about a necessary change . . . make the change.

God has a wonderful plan for you and wants to do amazing things in your life. All you have to do is trust Him and understand that His way is best.

SCRIPTURE TO MEDITATE ON TODAY

As for God, His way is perfect! . . . He is a shield to all those who take refuge and put their trust in Him.

PSALM 18:30

DAY 8

ONE DAY I WOKE UP with a throbbing headache. I thought maybe I was catching a cold. I walked around all day with that miserable headache, telling everybody I encountered how terrible I felt.

Finally, the Lord said to me, "Did it ever occur to you to ask Me to heal you?" I believed in Jesus as my Healer, but I had spent the day complaining and never once asked for healing.

> *In a season of transition, uncertainty or change, be bold enough to ask God to help you.*

Ask Him to teach you, to provide for you and to carry you through. The Bible says . . . *You do not have, because you do not ask* (James 4:2). So take some time to talk to the Lord today, telling Him how much you love Him and asking for His grace and provision.

What have you been complaining about rather than praying about?

Been Alone, Not Filting iN Anywhere.

PSALM 91:1 SAYS we can . . . *dwell in the secret place of the Most High.* That is such a wonderful promise because the secret place is the place of rest in God, a place of peace and comfort in Him.

> *This secret place is a "spiritual place" where worry vanishes and peace reigns.*

It is the place of God's presence. When we spend time praying, seeking God, and dwelling in His presence, we are in the secret place.

In other words, it's important that we are firmly planted in God. We need to know the source of our strength in every season of change. When God becomes our secret place, we can live in peace and security regardless of any storm we may face.

Spend some time alone with the Lord. Whether you pray about a specific need, worship or read the Word, seek God's presence and come into His "secret place."

DAY 10

ARE YOU SPENDING most of your time frustrated and worried? Would you say you enjoy your life, or are you letting difficult circumstances steal your joy?

If so, consider what the Bible says:
- *The joy of the Lord is your strength . . .*
  (NEHEMIAH 8:10)
- *A happy heart is good medicine . . .*
  (PROVERBS 17:22)
- *He will yet fill your mouth with laughter . . .*
  (JOB 8:21)

These verses (and so many others) teach us there is tremendous power in joy, happiness and laughter.

If you're going through a hard season, don't lose your joy. Take time to focus on God's blessings. Take time to laugh. Take time to have fun!

TRY THIS TODAY:

✓ *worry less*

✓ *laugh more*

✓ *repeat*

DAY 11

THE TOPIC OF "CONFIDENCE" is a popular one—both in the secular world and the church world.

Usually, when we're talking about confidence, people mean self-confidence. Self-confidence can be a good thing, but it's not the kind of confidence we really need.

> *The best kind of confidence is "God-confidence."*

More important than believing in ourselves, we need to believe in Christ, and how He can work in us and through us. Apart from Him, we can do nothing (see John 15:5). But with Him, there is nothing we cannot do (see Philippians 4:13).

In a season of change, when you feel uncertain or incapable of doing what you need to do, put your confidence in God. Because "God-confidence" will see you through every time!

Write your own personal prayer for today . . .

That I will GEt It!!
Know who I am in
Christ Jesus!!!
And to know I am open
to his purpose for my
Life,

DAY 12

IT'S SO EASY to be negative about life. In the midst of a frustrating day or a tough time, we often subconsciously begin to focus on what's wrong. *Life's not fair. This job is too hard. My kids are driving me crazy.*

> *But when we focus on the negative, it darkens our outlook and weakens our faith.*

So the next time negative thoughts cross your mind, take this simple action: Just say no! It's that easy. You can say *no* to the negative . . . and *yes* to the positive truth found in God's Word (see Colossians 3:2).

Instead of, *Life's not fair . . .* think, *My life is a blessing from God.* Instead of, *This job is too hard . . .* think, *Thank God I have a job.* Instead of, *My kids are driving me crazy . . .* think, *My kids may be a challenge, but I know God has great plans for their lives!*

QUESTION TO CONSIDER . . .

How different would
your life be if you took
time every day to choose
positive, joy-filled
thoughts that line up
with God's Word?

DAY 13

THE LONGER WE KNOW the Lord, the more relaxed we can become when we face situations that try to steal our peace. The experiences we go through with God are valuable because they teach us that somehow He always comes through.

Each time we face a new crisis, we can remember that, even though He may not have done exactly what we wanted Him to do, He always did the best thing for us to get us through it.

> *Relaxing in the face of trials helps us to maintain our peace with God.*

God wants us to trust Him and rest. I call this being *supernaturally relaxed* because in the natural, or naturally speaking, it's not easy to do. But when God adds His *super* to our *natural,* we end up with a supernatural rest in Him.

SCRIPTURE TO MEDITATE ON TODAY

Come to Me, all you who labor and are heavy-laden and overburdened, and I will cause you to rest. [I will ease and relieve and refresh your souls.]

MATTHEW 11:28

IT'S EASY TO BEGIN a new thing when you're excited about it. But it takes determination, perseverance, and sometimes great courage to finish.

In the beginning of a new thing, we have a lot of excited emotions (ours and everyone else's) to support us. But when the emotions wear off and all that is left is a lot of hard work and the need for extreme patience to see it through, we find out who really has what it takes to succeed.

> *If you've been tempted recently to give up—don't!*

If you don't finish the thing you are currently doing, you'll face the same challenge in the next thing you start. The only sure way to be successful is to see a thing through. Then one day, like the apostle Paul, you can say, *I have fought the good fight, I have finished the race, and I have remained faithful* (2 Timothy 4:7 NLT).

With God's help, you can finish your course . . . and you can do it with joy!

WISE WORDS

In the realm of ideas everything depends on enthusiasm . . . in the real world all rests on perseverance.

—JOHANN WOLFGANG VON GOETHE

THE BIBLE TELLS US repeatedly that God loves us, but so many of God's children still lack a true understanding, or revelation, concerning God's love for them.

The first time I prepared a message to teach outside the home Bible study I had been doing, I asked God what He wanted me to teach. He responded, "Tell My people that I love them." I thought that message was too simple, but God spoke to my heart, "Very few of My people really know how much I love them. If they did, they would act very differently than they do."

You may have a vague, general understanding that God loves you.

But I want to encourage you to really stop and think about what His Word says about His love for you . . .

God loves you. He gave His Son for you. You are never alone, abandoned or unloved. You have the unending, perfect love of your heavenly Father.

TRY THIS TODAY:

Look up the following scriptures and meditate on them to become more God-Loves-Me minded.

✓ *John 3:16-17*

✓ *1 John 4:7-11, 18-19*

DAY 16

THE WORD *MAGNIFY* means "to enlarge." When we tell God, "I magnify You," we are literally saying, *"God, I see You as bigger in my life than any problem, change or need that I have."*

Psalm 34:3 (AMP) says, *O magnify the Lord with me, and let us lift up His name together.* We are wise to magnify the Lord, seeing Him as larger than anything in our lives. When we worship and praise Him, we are doing just that. We are saying, "You are so big, so great, that I want to worship You."

By putting God first, we are taking our focus off our problems and putting our trust in God's promises.

I encourage you to magnify the Lord—not just when times are good, but also when things are uncertain. When you look to Him first, you'll be filled with faith and strength for the challenge at hand.

Put your faith in ACTION!

Write out three problems you are facing today . . . and then write "God" in big letters above them.

1. _____

2. _____

3. _____

LET THIS BE A REMINDER:
God is *bigger than* your problems!

DAY 17

IT'S EASY FOR someone to say, "Don't worry," but I don't think a person can fully overcome worry and fear—and develop habits of peace, rest and hope—without going through some experiences with God.

That's why it is so important to have faith and trust in God in the very midst of shifting, changing and tumultuous times.

Resist the temptation to give up and choose instead to spend time with God through prayer and reading His Word—embrace the experience you are in.

It is in this season that God is building in you the patience, endurance and character that will eventually produce the habit of joyful, confident hope. Take a few minutes to read Romans 5:1-5. Discover how hardships can be used by God to bring you greater peace, joy and hope.

Write your own personal prayer for today . . .

GOD LOVES YOU, and He's always with you, to help you in every area of your life, all the time. The truth is, we all need God; no one is smart enough to successfully run their life on their own. You don't have to go through life trying to fix your own problems. God is with you, and He is for you. You can depend on Him.

> *God cares about everything that concerns you—big and small.*

There is no concern, no frustration and no situation that is too insignificant for Him. You can take any problem to Him in this season of change, depending on Him to meet your need and give you the strength and courage to overcome.

Whenever you feel overwhelmed by your circumstances, mediate on Psalm 46:1, which says, *God is our refuge and strength [mighty and impenetrable], a very present and well-proved help in trouble* (AMP).

QUESTION TO CONSIDER . . .

If you stopped trying to solve all of your problems on your own and trusted God more, would you have more time, energy and happiness to share with family and friends?

WE ALL HAVE ROOM for improvement in our lives, and it's good to have goals to change and grow. It's important to understand that the transformations many people desire in different areas of their lives come through forming a pattern of obeying God in the little things. For example . . .

He may ask you to create more time in your schedule to relax.

He may ask you to seek someone's forgiveness. He may ask you to change your attitude about a particular person or situation.

Whatever it is, the more consistent you are in listening for God's voice and then obeying His promptings, the sooner the work will be done in you for the transformation to be complete.

SCRIPTURE TO MEDITATE ON TODAY

If you are willing and obedient, you shall eat the good of the land.

ISAIAH 1:19

ARE YOU TIRED OF the same-old circumstances and conditions in your life? Do you want something new? Then it's time to start speaking new things over your life.

Spend some time with God, studying His Word so you can find out what His will is for your life in this new season. Then make a conscious decision to come into agreement with the things He puts in your heart.

> *Don't listen to the enemy's lies or let your situation intimidate you.*

Find out what God promises you in His Word and begin to make new, faith-filled declarations.

Instead of saying, "I'll never survive this change," declare, "God is doing something new in my life." Meditate on Isaiah 43:18 -19 today. Get excited about His plan and purpose for this new season in your life!

What are some new declarations you can speak over your life today that are based on God's Word?

_____

_____

_____

_____

_____

_____

_____

DAY 21

WE ARE ASSURED and know that . . . *all things work together and are [fitting into a plan] for good to and for those who love God and are called according to [His] design and purpose* (Romans 8:28).

> *This scripture does not say that all things are good, but it does say that all things work together for good.*

When you're in the middle of a season of change—whether it's career change, relationship change, or new season of life—it may not always look like everything is good, but you can be sure that God is in control.

No matter what the circumstances look like, God can, and will, work them together for your good as you put your trust in Him. Just believe His Word, stand in faith and refuse to give up. When you do, you are going to see God do something amazing!

TRY THIS TODAY:

Decide to view your situation
in a whole new way:

a preparation for something GOOD God is doing in your life!

DAY 22

IT IS IMPORTANT FOR us to understand that when God does not move in our circumstances, or when He does not move as quickly as we would like for Him to move, He may be waiting on purpose.

> *God has a plan for your life, and He always accomplishes that plan in His timing.*

Maybe you're thinking there's no way you can get out of the mess you're in. That's the perfect time for God to . . . *show Himself strong in behalf of those whose hearts are blameless toward Him . . .* (2 Chronicles 16:9).

Remember that God's timing is always perfect. He knows exactly what you need . . . exactly when you need it. So when you're going through challenges in your life, don't worry. God is never late—He's always right on time!

Write your own personal prayer, asking God to help you trust His timing in your life . . .

TIMES OF CHANGE can be stressful and intense, especially when we don't know what to expect or we're uncertain of the future. Sometimes the best thing we can do is calm down and lighten up. Here are three ways to do that . . .

1. *Laugh more and worry less*

2. *Love more and judge less*

3. *Stop ruining today worrying about tomorrow*

The next time you are tempted to get anxious or upset about something during the transitions of life, make the decision at that moment to calm down and lighten up! With a joyful attitude, think about what you are doing and turn your mind to what is going on today.

Refuse to let fear of the unknown steal the joy of living in the present!

SCRIPTURE TO MEDITATE ON TODAY

May the God of your hope so fill you with all joy and peace in believing [through the experience of your faith] that by the power of the Holy Spirit you may abound and be overflowing (bubbling over) with hope.

ROMANS 15:13

DAY 24

FEAR IS A FEELING that causes negative reactions. It causes us to tremble, sweat, panic, shake, etc. The Bible doesn't say, "Shake not," or "Tremble not"—the Bible instructs us to "Fear not." And the word *fear* implies running from something.

In other words, God is saying when fear comes, which it always will, don't let it stop you. You can *do it afraid*!

> *Many people are*
> *afraid of change.*

We like things to stay the same, and when they don't, we get worried and afraid. If you're going through that today, don't freeze in your tracks or turn and retreat when you feel fear. Keep moving forward,

despite that fear, with your focus on God—do it afraid!
That is what will make the difference between victory
or defeat in your life.

TRY THIS TODAY:

Look up the following scriptures and
meditate on them whenever fear, worry
and anxiety try to overwhelm you:

√ *Psalm 118:6*

√ *Hebrews 13:6*

√ *Philippians 4:6-7*

MEDITATING ON OUR PROBLEMS, or the mistakes we've made in dealing with those problems, weakens us. But meditating on God's Word, His love for us, and His power and desire to help us gives us strength. We need to have a relationship and fellowship *with God*, not with our problems or our limitations.

> *How much time do you spend worrying about the uncertainty of change?*

Whatever amount of time that is . . . it's wasted, fruitless time. Instead of wasting time focused on the problem, spend time focused on the solution!

Don't allow your situation to pull your focus and attention off God. Instead of running *from* God in times of trouble, run *to* Him. If you'll be determined to draw closer to God in times of uncertainty, transition and change, you'll find peace in the storm and hope for a victorious outcome.

SCRIPTURE TO MEDITATE ON TODAY

Come close to God and He will come close to you.

JAMES 4:8

DAY 26

IN A SEASON OF CHANGE, it's easy to sit back and do nothing out of fear that you'll do the wrong thing. However, I encourage you to ask God for His direction and then respond with action as He leads you. James 1:5 says that if we ask Him for wisdom, He will give it to us . . . *generously and without rebuke or blame* (AMP).

> *Learning to hear from God is a process, and no one does it without making mistakes.*

Don't be overly concerned about errors. Learn from your mistakes, correct the ones you can, and continue being decisive.

A decisive person accomplishes a lot more with less effort. Don't fall back into a pattern of indecision and double-mindedness. If you feel God is prompting you to give something away, develop a new friendship, go in a different direction—do it! If you believe it is right, take action and go for it. That is how you will find out for sure.

What is a decisive action you could make today that you've been putting off?

DAY 27

IN ORDER TO FLOURISH and thrive in seasons of change, we need to have a sense of triumph or success. Romans 8:37 assures us that . . . *we are more than conquerors . . . through Him Who loved us.*

> *Sometimes our confidence is shaken when trials come, especially if they are lengthy.*

But we can have so much confidence in God's love for us that no matter what comes against us, we know deep inside that we can overcome any obstacle.

If you are truly confident in God, you have no need to fear trouble, challenges, trying times or change.

These things will pass, but God's love and goodness in your life never will. He is always with you, and because of that truth, you are more than a conqueror!

Put your faith in ACTION!

Look up Romans 8:37, write it down, and take several opportunities throughout the day to read it, thanking God that you are more than a conqueror in Christ Jesus!

DAY 28

SEEKING GOD continually is the best thing we can do, and when we're going through changes, it will keep us stable. Matthew 7:7 says, *Keep on asking and it will be given you; keep on seeking and you will find* . . .

I have learned that the word *seek* means to "pursue, crave, and go after with all your might." And that is something we need to do all the time, not just when we are in trouble.

> *We should seek God in the good times and the bad.*

I remember when God spoke this to my heart: "Seek Me as if you were desperate all the time, and then you won't find yourself in truly desperate situations as often."

This is good advice when we are in seasons of change. It may be tough; it may be easy. It may be the best thing you've gone through, or it may be the worst. Either way, seek God and He will fill your life with peace and joy for the journey.

QUESTION TO CONSIDER . . .

If you began seeking God with all of your heart, would your current situation be something that actually helps bring you closer to Him?

NO MATTER HOW DIFFICULT

your current circumstances are, don't give up!

In Galatians 6:9 (NIV), the apostle Paul says, *Let us not become weary in doing good, for at the proper time we will reap a harvest if we do not give up.* In other words, he's telling us to keep on keeping on!

> *Don't be a quitter!*
> *Choose to be a person who*
> *is bold enough to keep going.*

God is looking for people who will go all the way through with Him. Whatever you may be facing or experiencing right now in your life, I want to encourage you to go through it and not give up! It's easy to quit—it takes faith to stick it out and go all the way to the finish.

You can do it as you trust God and lean on His grace— not your own strength or ability—to get where you need to be.

SCRIPTURE TO MEDITATE ON TODAY

Let us not lose heart and grow weary and faint in acting nobly and doing right, for in due time . . . we shall reap, if we do not loosen and relax our courage and faint.

GALATIANS 6:9

65

THE DESIRE TO take care of ourselves is based on fear. Basically, it stems from the idea that if *we* do it, we can be sure it will be done right. We are afraid of what might happen if we entrust ourselves totally to God and He doesn't "come through" for us.

> *The root problem of self-reliance is trusting ourselves more than we trust God.*

We may say we're trusting God, but at the same time, we have a backup plan. We may pray and ask God to get involved in our lives, but if He is the least bit slow in responding (at least, to our way of thinking), we are quick to take control back into our own hands.

What we fail to realize is, God has a plan for us too—
and His plan is much better than ours.

In any season of change, resist the urge to take control.
Rely on God, rather than yourself, and trust that His
plan for your life is best!

*Read Proverbs 3:5-6 and write your own
personal prayer for today . . .*

CONGRATULATIONS

ON COMPLETING

THIS 30-DAY

SURVIVAL GUIDE!

Your monthlong journey of learning to trust God more through times of change has hopefully brought you closer to Him and given you more peace and joy.

But we want to encourage you not to stop there. God has so much more in store for you, and it's important for you to keep moving forward with Him each day.

We want to help you do that, so we have created a free, tailor-made experience that will encourage, strengthen and help you go deeper in God's Word at your own pace. Go to **joycemeyer.org/biblestudy** and you'll discover several options to choose from.

No matter where you are in your relationship with God, you'll find a study plan that's right for you. Establishing the God-habit is the best decision you can make!

For I know the thoughts and plans that I have for you, says the Lord, thoughts and plans for welfare and peace and not for evil, to give you hope in your final outcome.

JEREMIAH 29:11